SWITCH OFF

SWITCH OFF

The Clergy Guide to Preserving
Energy and Passion for Ministry

Heather Bradley
and Miriam Bamberger Grogan

Foreword by Steve and Cokie Roberts

Abingdon Press
Nashville

SWITCH OFF:
THE CLERGY GUIDE TO PRESERVING ENERGY AND PASSION FOR MINISTRY

Copyright © 2016 by Abingdon Press

All rights reserved.

Library of Congress Cataloging-in-Publication Data

Names: Bradley, Heather L., author.
Title: Switch off : the clergy guide to preserving energy and passion for
    ministry / Heather L. Bradley and Miriam B. Grogan.
Description: First [edition]. | Nashville, Tennessee : Abingdon Press,
2016.
    | Includes bibliographical references.
Identifiers: LCCN 2016021643 | ISBN 9781501810466 (pbk.)
Subjects: LCSH: Pastoral theology. | Clergy--Psychology.
Classification: LCC BV4011.3 .B73 2016 | DDC 253/.2--dc23
LC record available at https://lccn.loc.gov/2016021643

16 17 18 19 20 21 22 23 24 25—10 9 8 7 6 5 4 3 2 1
MANUFACTURED IN THE UNITED STATES OF AMERICA

CONTENTS

Foreword: Controlling the Chaos

By Steve and Cokie Roberts   vii

Preface   xi

Introduction   xiii

A Few Notes About This Book   xiii

How to Get the Most from This Book   xiv

PART I

What Is the Off Switch?   3

The Challenge   3

The Solution: The Off Switch   4

The Off-Switch Questions   5

Question #1: Where Am I Taking on Stuff That Isn't Mine?   6

What It Takes to Support a Congregation   7

Key Roles   8

Common Challenges When Working with Roles   10

Tool #1: Your Role Analysis   11

Question #2: How Much Is Enough?   21

How Do I Make Peace with Feeling That Whatever I Do Isn't Enough?   22

The Three Levels of Reality   22

The Three Levels in Congregational Life   23

Initiate Dialogue   25

Tool #2: Your Reality Check   27

Question #3: What Do I Need to Say Yes To? Say No To?   35

Tool #3: Your Boundary Analysis   37

Are You Focusing on What You Can Control?   40

Tool #4: Your Control Analysis   40

Your Personal Plan   42

Tool #5: Your Personal Action Plan for Finding and Using
   Your Off Switch   43

   SMART Goals   44

PART II

The Off-Switch Retreat   47

PART III

Your Personal Action Plan   81

   Tool #1: Your Role Analysis   83

   Tool #2: Your Reality Check   84

   Tool #3: Your Boundary Analysis   85

   Tool #4: Your Control Analysis   86

   Tool #5: Your Personal Action Plan   87

Conclusion   89

Acknowledgments   91

CONTROLLING THE CHAOS

By Steve and Cokie Roberts

Reading this eminently sane and sensible book reminds us of the famous Serenity Prayer written by the theologian Reinhold Niebuhr.

> God, grant me the serenity to accept the things I
> cannot change,
> Courage to change the things I can,
> And wisdom to know the difference.

Like Niebuhr, Heather Bradley and Miriam Grogan capture the paradox at the core of daily existence. To live a meaningful life you have to take control, set priorities, make a plan, and follow through. At the same time you have to acknowledge that all plans don't work out. Some things are beyond your control. There is wisdom in the Yiddish proverb: "Man plans and God laughs."

Bradley and Grogan have drawn on their long careers as executive coaches and applied their experience to the world of the clergy. They avoid doctrinal debates and focus on the ground-level, everyday lives of the pastors and ministers, the priests and rabbis and imams who manage the institutions that guide and support our spiritual lives.

This small volume is a passionate plea for clarity and balance, but it's much more than that. It's a practical guide on how to achieve that balance, how to serve others while preserving oneself.

Virtually every page contains useful insights leavened with humor. Take this catalog of identities that all ministers in all faiths have to assume: "Spiritual leader. Preacher. Teacher. Manager. Employer. Employee. Spouse. Parent. Child. Mentor. Student. Fund-raiser. Visionary. Person who mops up the puddles when the roof leaks."

The goal, they write, is to reconcile these roles without losing your focus or your freedom. They'll help you learn to make time for three essential practices—relaxing, reflecting, refreshing—while still giving your congregation all the devotion it deserves.

Every parent (we have two children and six grandchildren) knows the validity of this advice. Burnout is real. You can do your job well only if you hit the Off Switch regularly. Tuning out makes you better at tuning in.

We've never forgotten the moment in our young married lives when we had two small children at home and managed to escape for a romantic weekend. We were strolling down Fisherman's Wharf in San Francisco when Cokie turned to Steve and said, "Have an affair with your wife." The authors would heartily agree.

All these goals—sanity, balance, control—are easier to articulate than to achieve. But Bradley and Grogan are here to help. They teach as well as preach.

"Remember every action or reaction—even no action—is a choice," they write. "Every time we say yes to one thing, we say no to another. Likewise, if we say no to something, we say yes to something else. When we make conscious and intentional choices, we're better able to reclaim our sense of control."

Yes, God laughs when we humans make plans. But this is also true: pastors serve the Word and the world by bringing a "sense of control" out of chaos.

PREFACE

W hen we told people we were working on a book for clergy, the universal response was, "That's great!" When we asked why, we heard some version of, "We clergy need all the help we can get."

Clergy are part of a profession like no other. However you define it, the label *clergy* represents a collection of roles that come together in various combinations based on religion, congregational size, and congregational structure. Frustration can build when clergy think they are delivering what is expected of them and the feedback (formal or informal) they receive indicates that expectations are not being met. Worse, in the absence of feedback, clergy can be caught off guard if they assume everything is fine only to learn unexpectedly everything is not fine.

This book will help you examine the roles you inhabit and the roles of others around you. You will also be challenged to look at old problems in a new way, and we'll offer tools to help unwind the complexities of your personal situation and develop new habits to manage expectations.

Introduction

A Few Notes About This Book

Despite the fact that this book is written for religious professionals, you may be surprised to find it has a secular feel. This is intentional. We do not presume to offer guidance on how you discharge your religious duties and obligations.

Rather our goal is to offer you tools to manage the pressures of congregational life. We have not attempted to address every situation you might confront. The differences among denominations and congregational settings make that impossible. Instead we have focused on the commonalities faced by the religious professionals we interviewed. We have crafted vignettes based on themes we heard in these conversations. The tools introduced throughout this book can be applied to many of the situations you face.

Finally, in recognition of the wide variety of religions in America, and the increasing gender diversity in the clergy of some of these religions, we have used titles (minister, rabbi, pastor, and so on) and gender-specific pronouns (he, she) interchangeably. We urge you not to be distracted from the content by anything that is not appropriate to your denomination but rather to "translate" the text to a form that is most comfortable to you.

How to Get the Most from This Book

This book is divided into three parts.

Part 1 of the book provides an overview of the Off-Switch metaphor. Here you'll find the three critical questions for finding and using your Off Switch. Case vignettes, based on conversations with active congregational clergy, and coaching exercises help you explore the questions and understand how to use them effectively.

Part 2 of the book shows you how all three questions fit together through the story of a group of clergy who come together in a retreat setting to explore the topic of the Off Switch.

Part 3 provides you the opportunity to create your personal plan for finding and using your Off Switch and presents the model and all the tools in one place for easy reference.

All of the case vignettes, characters, and challenges are based on real-life experience. In fact, we heard several of these stories from different people, across denominations and geography.

As you read through these pages, we invite you to take your own personal journey. There are a number of ways to do this.

- You might read it straight through, as you would a novel or nonfiction book, perhaps noting concepts and tools you'd like to refer to later.

- As you read, you might stop along the way to do a few of the exercises.

- You might do a deep dive, reading each section thoroughly and doing all of the exercises.

- You might read one section every month, digesting the concepts and testing one tool at a time.

- You might work through it (in one of these ways) with a coach, friend, or group of colleagues.

- You might come up with a completely different way of using it. (Please let us know!)

In whatever way you use this book, we hope it will help you reconnect with what truly matters for you and turn off those things that are interfering with your satisfaction.

May the lessons in these pages help you relax, reflect, and refresh. In other words, may you find and use your Off Switch.

PART I

WHAT IS THE
OFF SWITCH?

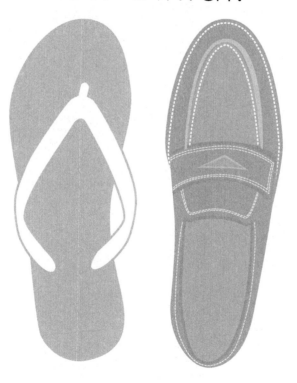

WHAT IS
THE OFF SWITCH?

I lie awake at night thinking of my congregants. How are they doing? How can I help them?

    My friends are uncomfortable with my role—they grew
up thinking the pastor is untouchable. I have to make them feel
comfortable.

    No one taught us to read contracts or manage staff in seminary.

Sound familiar? As we began interviewing members of the
clergy about this book, a few concerns began to emerge.

The Challenge

As a member of the clergy, you occupy a special place in
our society. You come to the role to serve, and in many cases,
you may be asked to serve twenty-four hours a day, seven days
a week. This passion and caring are inspiring but potentially
exhausting.

Even the most energetic congregational leader has limited
energy. Structured free time, such as a weekly day off or a pe-
riodic sabbatical, are a great start, but they may not always be
practical. And even if you are able to enjoy time off the clock,
now and then your mind can drift back to your role!

The Solution: The Off Switch

Like a lightbulb, if you don't allow yourself to turn off from time to time, burnout will catch up with you. Finding your Off Switch means identifying the issues that keep you On, examining them in a fresh light, and giving yourself permission to address them in a way that will allow you to relax and refresh. To re-soul, if you will.

As we sifted through our interview notes, we came to the Off Switch metaphor as we noticed three themes floating in the background of every conversation.

- My work never ends.

- Whatever I do, it's never enough.

- I have to do it all.

Figure 1 — Concerns Preventing Access to Your Off Switch

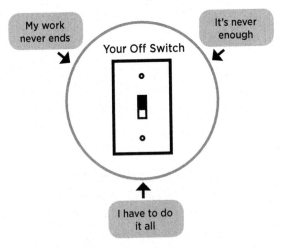

The Off-Switch Questions

As coaches, we've seen over and over how useful questions lead us to challenge our assumptions and open up new possibilities. So we've flipped the identified themes into questions to consider.

1. Where am I taking on stuff that isn't mine?

2. How much is enough?

3. What do I need to say yes to? What do I need to say no to?

Figure 2 – Turning Concerns into Questions

Expressed Concern	Off-Switch Question
My work never ends.	Q1. Where am I taking on stuff that isn't mine?
It's never enough.	Q2. How much is enough?
I have to do it all	Q3. What do I need to say yes to? Say no to?

The Off-Switch questions create an opportunity to address these concerns, allowing you to shine your light on a greater vision of what is possible from your pulpit.

Figure 3 — Off-Switch Questions

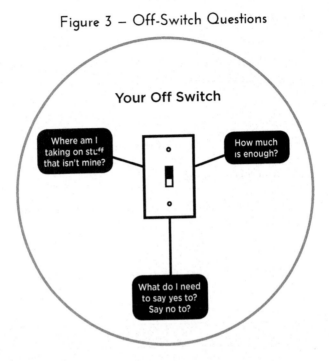

Question #1 : Where Am I Taking on Stuff That Isn't Mine?

Where does a minister's job begin and end? This is not the beginning of a joke. It's a serious question, often with no clear answers. Each congregation and each congregant are different, with different ideas of what their spiritual leader should be doing. With unclear boundaries and often incompatible expectations, it's no wonder clergy and congregants can be confused about the pastor's role!

It's nice to think that as educated adults, we know truth from fiction; we see situations as they are, not as we'd like them to be. In reality, we all make things up.

In the absence of clear, agreed-upon expectations for a minister, all the players—congregants, staff, the minister's family, even the minister himself!—make up different interpretations of what is expected. Many of the clergy we spoke to were taking on other people's work, either others' formal responsibilities or the nice little extras that weren't really anybody's job. Without a clear of sense of where their jobs began and ended, our interviewees had no idea how to find an Off Switch and when to use it. Most felt a level of frustration; many reported suffering from lack of sleep and other health issues.

The first tool for finding the Off Switch is to clarify where you're taking on stuff that isn't yours. With new insights from using these tools, you may still decide to take on some stuff that isn't yours, but it will happen by choice, not by accident.

What It Takes to Support a Congregation

The job of clergy is complicated: Spiritual leader. Preacher. Teacher. Manager. Employer. Employee. Spouse. Parent. Child. Mentor. Student. Fund-raiser. Visionary. Person who mops up the puddles when the roof leaks.

We could probably spend the whole book listing roles and barely scratch the surface. Rather than attempt to come up with a comprehensive list, let's talk about three categories of roles that most affect the group dynamics. We see these types of roles in project teams, corporations, families, interpersonal conflict—in other words, just about everywhere. We will use the term *system* in this discussion to apply to any group of two or more; primarily, but not limited to, a congregation.[1]

1. We are grateful to CRR Global, developers of Organization and Relationship Systems Coaching (ORSC) model. The following is adapted from the roles framework detailed in its program.

7

Key Roles

Outer roles define the structure of a system and are often identified by job title, such as executive director, rector, or treasurer. Outer roles may also reference a set of tasks, such as note-taker or snack provider. Outer roles dictate our job functions and are important for clarity and efficiency.

> *Outer roles answer the question*
> *"Who does what?"*

Inner roles point to the emotional functioning of the system and may or may not have anything to do with individuals' outer roles. They often express values needed by the system. Examples of inner roles are devil's advocate, cheerleader, initiator, peacemaker.

> *Inner roles answer the question*
> *"How do we work together?"*

Ghost roles are third-party presences that come and go. They can be positive or negative. While not physically present, ghosts exert a powerful influence, whether or not the system members address them. There are three types of ghosts: people, circumstances, and culture.

People ghosts include people who have been members of your congregational system (i.e., the beloved senior pastor who led your church for twenty-five years and is now retired) or those who have not been a member of your immediate system but have an influence (i.e., the pope in the Roman Catholic Church).

Circumstantial ghosts include specific events impacting the congregation, such as a 150th anniversary, a project such as the leaky roof in the sanctuary, or the death of an influential congregant.

Cultural ghosts are societal influences, such as racism, homophobia, sexism, ageism, or discrimination against people with disabilities. Cultural ghost roles are often long established and they exist beyond a specific congregational system, affecting not only a congregation, but also broader society.

All three types of ghost roles help explain what is going on below the surface. And because they operate below the surface, they can be a challenge to identify and address. If your work with outer and inner roles does not yield the changes you want, ghosts may be operating in your system.

> *Ghost roles answer the question*
> *"What forces exist but cannot be observed*
> *directly?"*

Figure 4 – Key Roles

Roles	Purpose
Outer roles	Who does what?
Inner roles	How do we work together?
Ghost roles	What forces exist but cannot be observed directly?

Common Challenges When Working with Roles

To see where, or if, you are taking on stuff that isn't yours, examine the following aspects of roles that commonly cause disruptions.

Roles are not people. When people occupy a role for a long time, they often become identified by it. Roles are essentially a collection of tasks required to maintain the effective operation of the system, not the people who do those tasks.

Figure 5 – Finding and Using Your Off Switch: Key Roles

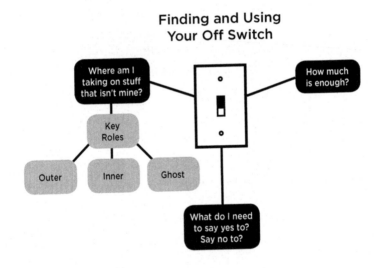

Tool #1: Your Role Analysis

Role Identification
List all of your outer roles.
List all of your inner roles.
What ghosts are affecting your role/congregation?
Where have you become too closely identified with a role?
Poorly Occupied Roles
Role Confusion
Role Changes
Role Nausea
Where are you taking on stuff that isn't yours due to role challenges?

Case Vignette

Ellen is the music director, and in this position, she leads the youth choir. Three of the children live in Ellen's neighborhood, so she drives them home, happy for the company and to save the parents an extra trip. After several months, Ellen wants to establish a teen choir that would practice after the youth choir, but she feels she can't: she has come to see herself as her role, the driver. Collapsing the role of driver into the role of youth choir director limits her opportunities.

On the flip side, when a person becomes too identified with a role, others may feel excluded from participating or even learning about it. Adam is the father of one of the kids Ellen drives. Adam would like to take on the role of after-choir driver to spend more time with his daughter and her friends. But Adam doesn't want to offend Ellen; he doesn't want her to think they don't appreciate her driving or that he's muscling in on her territory.

The fact of this situation is that the children in the choir need safe transportation to and from choir activities. Driver is the outer role. Ellen currently occupies the role of driver. Everything else is made up. Ellen is working from assumptions about what is expected of her and what will happen if she no longer occupies the outer role of driver. Adam is unsure what Ellen's reaction will be if he initiates a change in this outer role. We don't know, but there could also be a ghost of the previous youth choir director. Or Adam could be influenced by a cultural ghost; when Adam was growing up, dads didn't typically drive their children to and from activities.

Ask yourself:

• What roles are you identified by that could be filled by others?

Roles are poorly occupied or badly performed. As we discussed in the previous section, the person is not the role. Rather a role, outer or inner, is populated by someone. What happens if the person filling the role is not fully qualified or prepared to fulfill the needed requirements? Or the incumbent is not performing the role well? Often a member of the clergy ends up taking it on, and using the Off Switch gets pushed further back on the to-do list.

Ask yourself:

• What roles are poorly occupied in your system?

• Which incumbents are not performing their roles well?

• Where are you taking on stuff that isn't yours because a role is poorly occupied or the incumbent is performing badly?

Roles confuse more than clarify. Role confusion exists when we don't know, or have lost track of, who does what. Role confusion can creep into a system or drop in with a big thud, and it can occur for several reasons.

Figure 6 — Symptoms and Causes of Outer Role Confusion

Outer Role Confusion	
Some Symptoms	Cause
• Duplicate effort • Missed tasks and deadlines • Lack of accountability	• Lack of clarity about the required work and who is accountable for doing the work • Unqualified person doing the work

Figure 7 — Symptoms and Causes of Inner Role Confusion

Inner Role Confusion	
Some Symptoms	Cause
• Clashes • Lack of productivity • Role not filled	• Lack of awareness of inner roles

Many people tend toward certain kinds of inner roles. For example, most clergy (outer role) have an affinity for relater or communicator inner roles, and they probably have less affinity for being disciplinarians.

Figure 8 — Symptoms and Causes of Role Creep

Role Creep	
Some Symptoms	Cause
• Roles expand organically • Lines between outer roles blur	• Incumbent feels he/she can't say no • Onetime event becomes the norm • Role reviews do not occur • Emerging roles are not identified/planned for

Case Vignette

Bill and Greg are both associate pastors at their growing church. Not long after they arrived, the two men and the senior pastor met to discuss how to divide the many responsibilities. They quickly came up with a list that balanced their individual interests with the church needs. Among Greg's outer roles is the bank run. The church is participating in a fund-raising drive for the local food shelter; checks are arriving each day, so the daily bank run has taken on additional importance. Greg occasionally grouses to his best friend—after all, Greg is a minister, not a clerk. But he knows it is important for the church, and he does live near the bank's main branch.

One day, Greg has a meeting on the other side of town and fears he won't be back before the branch closes. He knocks on Bill's office door. "Would you mind doing the bank run today?" Greg asks, explaining the situation.

"I'd be happy to," says Bill, taking the deposit. "I'm going to the hospital to visit Mrs. Jones, so it's right on my way."

A few days later, in the staff meeting, the senior pastor mentions that Mr. Smith has gone into the hospital. "I can see him this afternoon," Bill offers.

"Oh, would you mind stopping at the bank on the way?" Greg asks. Bill says he wouldn't mind at all.

This could be the end of the story. Bill occasionally steps into Greg's outer role when necessary. After all, colleagues help one another all the time.

Or it could be the beginning of role creep, if Bill allows this piece of Greg's role to morph into an extra, permanent aspect of his (Bill's) role.

Ask yourself:

- Where are you taking on someone else's stuff as a favor—more than once?

- Where do you see role creep in your organization?

- Where are you taking on someone else's stuff because of role creep?

Roles change. Congregations are dynamic systems. Some roles, once crucial, may no longer be necessary and need to be retired. Perhaps the congregation had a switchboard, but the new automated system has made the operator role obsolete.

16

By contrast, new roles may emerge. For example, most congregations have a social media presence these days. The role of social media manager almost certainly didn't exist when most of you went to seminary, but it is critical now!

Ask yourself:

- What roles need to be retired?

- What needs are emerging and require the creation of a new role?

- Where are you taking on stuff that isn't yours, either by filling roles that need to be retired or assuming emerging roles that need to be filled by someone else?

Role nausea infects the team. Role nausea is the feeling of being sick and tired of a role. We can easily imagine Ellen, the choir director, saying, "If I have to take these screaming kids home one more time…!" In truth, she may love the role; she just needs a break today. Like physical nausea, role nausea passes relatively quickly; it's not a chronic disease. The solution is to see if the role can go unfilled for a short time, or if Ellen can find a temporary replacement. Just be sure the substitute's tenure is clearly spelled out so role confusion doesn't inadvertently crop up or role creep set in.

Ask yourself:

- For which of your roles have you developed role nausea?

- What would provide relief?

- Who around you has developed role nausea?

- Where are you taking on someone else's stuff to ease their role nausea?

Figure 9 — Finding and Using Your Off Switch: Role Challenges

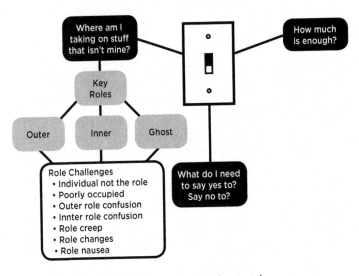

Finding and Using Your Off Switch

Where am I taking on stuff that isn't mine?

How much is enough?

Key Roles

Outer · Inner · Ghost

Role Challenges
• Individual not the role
• Poorly occupied
• Outer role confusion
• Innter role confusion
• Role creep
• Role changes
• Role nausea

What do I need to say yes to? Say no to?

Figure 10 — Ellen's Role Analysis

Remember Ellen? She is the youth choir director who drives the kids home. The following chart shows how she might analyze her roles and attitudes toward them.

Role Identification
List all of your outer roles.
• Music Director
• Youth choir leader
• Adult choir leader
• Teacher
• Conductor
• Driver

List all of your inner roles.
- Person everyone can count on
- Shoulder to cry on

What ghosts are affecting your role/congregation?
"Good" church staff do everything asked of them—and more. I think people expect me to be the driver. Whether it's kids or Mrs. Jones, who lives in my neighborhood, they expect me to schlep everyone, regardless of my other obligations.

Where have you become too closely identified with a role?
Driver, person everyone can count on.

Poorly Occupied Roles
Truth teller: we don't like but we don't always say how we really feed because we don't want to be hurtful or unhelpful.

Role Confusion
When am I the driver? I don't mind when it's convenient, but who will fill it when I'm not available?

Role Changes
We need to retire "assumer." Everyone assumes we like things the way they are.

Role Nausea
I'm sick of being the regular driver. It would actually be kind of fun if I didn't have to do it all the time.

Where are you taking on stuff that isn't yours due to role challenges?
I'm taking on the role of driver because with my inner role as "a person others can count on," I think it's rude to say no or let people down.

Figure 11 — Bill's Role Analysis

Remember Bill? He took the bank run as a favor to Greg. Here is his role analysis.

Role Identification
List all of your outer roles. • Preacher • Teacher • Visitor of sick • Funeral leader • Service leader
List all of your inner roles. • Peacemaker • Connector • Comforter • Conflict avoider • Greg's lackey
What ghosts are affecting your role/congregation? Everyone helps out. Associate pastors are best friends.
Where have you become too closely identified with a role? The ghost that says associate pastors are best friends. Greg's OK, but I wouldn't be friends with him if we didn't work together.
Poorly Occupied Roles Obviously Greg's role as bank runner.

Role Confusion
When is it OK for me to have the role of "person who pushes back"?
Why Greg thinks it's OK to avoid doing part of his job.
Role Changes
We need to retire Greg's role of "buck passer."
Role Nausea
I'm sick of being Greg's lackey.
Where are you taking on stuff that isn't yours due to role challenges?
I'm realizing I've made "peace keeper" my role. I'm taking on Greg's responsibility to keep the peace.

Question #2: How Much Is Enough?

The role of clergy has few metrics, another reason the Off Switch can be so elusive. How many visits to the hospital are "enough"? How many revisions of a sermon are "enough"? How many conversations with congregants are "enough"? Without useful answers to questions like these, our Off Switch can go haywire.

"How much is enough?" is a one-dimensional question for a multifaceted dilemma; the question isn't useful because it doesn't match the problem. Rather than try to answer the unanswerable question, consider "How much is enough?" as a doorway to a series of more useful questions, ultimately including: How do I make peace with feeling that whatever I do isn't enough?

So let's start over.

*How Do I Make Peace with Feeling That Whatever I Do Isn't
Enough?*

First, recognize you have a lot of company. "It's never
enough" is a common refrain, both among the clergy and also
in the civilian population. We use a framework crystallized by
psychologists Arny and Amy Mindell: the three levels of reality
that help sort out the tensions that exist.[2]

We often deal with people who have a different concept of
reality from ours. The Mindells' model helps us see that navigating the personalities and challenges of a congregation often
leads to navigating different levels of "reality." Although most
of us have a preferred level of reality, we find important insights
as we travel among them and gather information from each
level.

The Three Levels of Reality

Everyday level of reality. Since this is the level where most
"doing" takes place, it is the easiest level to identify: proofread-
ing bulletins, asking the janitor to replace the lightbulb...or
doing it yourself. To-do lists and time lines are tools commonly
used on this level of reality.

Strategic level of reality. On this level, tasks are not com-
pleted but plans, such as budgets or membership-drive targets,
are created. Visions of what we can become are born. Hopes
and fears operate on this level.

Fundamental level of reality. This level holds what is essential to each of us, the values, passion, and purpose of an
individual or organization. This level infuses our congregations

---

2. The framework presented here is adapted from the work of Arny and Amy
Mindell, originally presented to the authors in the ORSC program.

(and us!) with the vitality that is the very core of who we are and binds us together. It's the spark that enlivens us, the intangible spirit distinguishing our congregation from the one down the street.

Figure 12 – Finding and Using Your Off Switch:
Levels of Reality

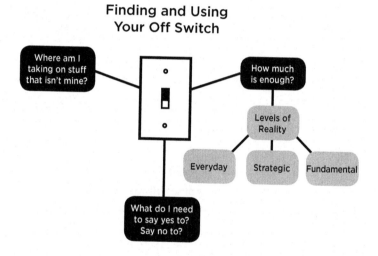

The Three Levels in Congregational Life

Feeling overwhelmed usually manifests in everyday reality, where "How much is enough?" refers to action: how many visits, conversations, and so on.

But the root of the problem is typically turmoil at another level, such as frustration and burnout that come from chasing goals that aren't part of a larger vision (strategic) or grounded in meaningful purpose (fundamental).

The strategic level of reality is where we define visions and design plans; "How much is enough?" points us to direction. In other words, am I satisfied with where my vision and plans are taking me? As a congregation, are we satisfied with where our visions and plans are taking us? While many congregations take the time to articulate a vision and establish a strategic plan to accomplish it, few individuals take the time to do this important strategic contemplation for themselves.

The fundamental level of reality causes us to consider meaning. What's important about what we're doing? Does our congregation stand for enough? While the metrics of everyday reality are easy to identify (although sometimes difficult to articulate), we suspect the conversations at the fundamental level of reality, relating as they do to values, passion, and mission, are easiest for us to access. Indeed, this is the level of most spiritual conversations.

Figure 13 – Indicators for Feelings of "Not Enough"

Level of Reality	Indicator	Question
Everyday	Action	What needs to be done?
Strategic	Direction	Where am I heading?
Fundamental	Meaning	What is important about this?

All three levels are important, and in fact each of us needs to move among all of them. If we focus only on prayer and our way of being (fundamental), earthly work isn't accomplished (everyday). And unless we infuse the tasks of everyday reality with our values and passion on a meaningful path, we head toward frustration and burnout.

Our secular society focuses on *doing*: What are you going to do? What have you done for me lately? So it is tempting to begin a to-do list in everyday reality. But with so many needs pulling you in different directions, and with the "How much is enough?" measurement challenges we've already discussed, actions are important, but not, in our view, the right place to start.

The first step is to pause and identify, or reconnect, with what's important: your values, your purpose. This clarity will help you decide what tasks go on your to-do list, and the priority they deserve.

Of course, this is only half of the equation. Other people, staff, congregants, family, and community members all have opinions of how much is enough from you, and others' expectations are directly related to Off Switch challenges. Their assumptions, stated or not, and their preferred levels of reality can contribute to your uneasiness in trying to answer how much is enough.

Initiate Dialogue

One strategy for addressing challenges about how much is enough and levels of reality is to initiate dialogue with the others involved. You may not be able to change anything in everyday reality, but the fundamental and strategic level experiences of all the participants can shift dramatically.

As a result, you might be able to use your Off Switch to enjoy a few minutes of downtime, confident in the knowledge that staff members understand what is being asked and are able to make an informed response.

When our Off Switch is broken or missing, it's easy to forget the power of dialogue. We know you can come up with a million great questions. Here are a few to help you initiate the dialogue if you get stuck.

- What do you need from me?

- How would you like to see this unfold?

- In your perfect world, how would this work out?

- What's your biggest fear/concern around this?

Figure 14 – Finding and Using Your Off Switch: Indicators

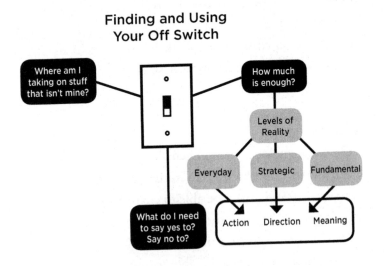

Tool #2: Your Reality Check

List the many parts of your outer and inner roles where it seems as if, no matter what you do, it's not enough.			
Pick one to explore further. Issue:			
Level of Reality	Indicator	Question	What you are noticing
As you look at the issue now, what do you see that you didn't see before?			
What is the next step?			

Case Vignette #1

Robert is the associate rabbi at his temple. Youthful and energetic, he's tasked with reaching out to young professionals, creating new programs to draw them in, and helping them find their place in the established congregation. Of course, this is in addition to all of his other responsibilities. Robert's preferred level of reality is everyday; he is efficient and a great manager of time. He has a detailed to-do list and regularly crosses everything off in the time he's planned for it.

Deidre is the temple president. Her preferred level of reality is strategic. She is a management consultant, and helping clients with strategy is her dream job come true. She brings her love of high-level thinking to her responsibilities at the temple. She adores Robert—his energy and excitement are infectious. But she is frustrated with him. His sermons are original and inspired, but he doesn't bring the same creativity to his young-professional outreach work. She has suggested several new program ideas; he takes copious notes but never discusses the suggestions with her and does not take the steps necessary to implement them. She decides to say something to David, the senior rabbi.

One evening on his way out, David pokes his head into Robert's office. David mentions he's just been meeting with Deidre, prompting Robert to slump into a chair. "I know this is a—ahem—'growth opportunity' for me," Robert says with evident sarcasm. "But I find her so frustrating. She has all of these great ideas, but she has no inkling of what it takes to put on these programs: the time, the volunteer coordination, the staff time, not to mention the money. I know she's annoyed with me, but she just doesn't get it. Her pie-in-the-sky ideas just aren't practical."

Figure 15 — Robert's Reality Check

List the many parts of your outer and inner roles where it seems as if, no matter what you do, it's not enough.

1. Outreach: Deidre always wants more.
2. Programs: They're never original or interesting enough for Deidre.
3. Speaking up to Deidre. No matter what I say, she doesn't listen.

Pick one to explore further in each level of reality.

Issue: #1 Outreach: No matter what I do, it isn't enough for Deidre.

Level of Reality	Indicator	Question	What you are noticing?
Fundamental	Meaning	What is important about this?	What's important is modeling good working relationships for the rest of the congregation, establishing good programs to help us grow, and my sanity!

Strategic	Direction	Where am I headed?	We're headed for a stalemate. We need to be headed toward a shared vision of the congregation. Actually, I think we want a lot of the same things, we just have different ideas of how they'll play out.
Everyday	Action	What needs to be done?	I need to figure out a way to talk with Deidre without getting upset, where I can listen and state my points clearly. Maybe ask my college friend who is a management consultant for "consultant-speak."

As you look at _outreach_ now, what do you see that you didn't see before?

I need to have a conversation with Deidre about how we evaluate new ideas or approaches.

What is the next step?

- Schedule time by the end of the week to draft a possible process and criteria to evaluate new ideas or approaches.

- Schedule time with David at the beginning of next week to solicit his perspective and suggestions on the draft. I also want to enroll David as an ally for this approach.

- Schedule time with Deidre by the end of next week to review the proposed process and the need for a more structured approach.

- Circle back with David, share Deidre's comments, and propose the recommended process be added to the agenda for review at the next leadership meeting.

Case Vignette #2

Benjamin is a priest. One of Benjamin's favorite parts of his outer role is visiting the sick. Someone with a broken leg, a parishioner entering hospice, or parents of a sick child: Benjamin has a special knack for these situations. He knows he brings comfort to the patients and their families, and he always feels good when leaves.

To keep visits with the sick from taking all of his time (which he'd love to see happen), Benjamin limits himself to visiting the hospital on Tuesdays and the nursing home on Thursdays, unless a parishioner specifically asks him to come another time or there is an emergency. He has this guideline clearly detailed on his web page and publishes it each week in the bulletin. Clear parameters and communication have helped him make peace with his everyday reality policy.

When Benjamin greets worshippers after mass one Sunday, Carol, an active congregant, is barely polite. The mechanics of her greeting are all perfectly scripted, but her demeanor indicates she is furious with Benjamin. He is baffled about what he has done.

Benjamin tries to talk with her during the Fellowship Hour, both in a group and by themselves, but Carol is having none of it. He calls her during the week, but she doesn't return his calls.

Finally they happen to be the only ones in the church office one evening. "Carol," Benjamin calls. She starts to leave but he catches up with her. "Have I done something to offend you? I apologize if I have, but for the life of me, I don't know what it is."

"Father," Carol says curtly. She starts to huff something but stops, her eyes welling up with tears. "Father," she continues, this time quietly. "My mother has been in the hospital for a month...." Her voice trails off. After a minute, Benjamin decides she is waiting for him to speak.

"Yes, I know," he says gently. "I've seen her every week since she's been in. Of course, you were there the first time, then she was asleep the second time, so I left a note. And then last week she and I had a very nice visit." He waits to see what Carol will say.

"That's just it. You've only been to see her three times. How can you possibly think it's enough?"

Figure 16 – Benjamin's Reality Check

List the many parts of your outer and inner roles where it seems as if, no matter what you do, it's not enough.

- Writing sermons—I know I could reach people in a more meaningful way if I had more time to revise and practice them
- Supervising the office staff
- Visiting the sick
- Counseling parishioners

Pick one to explore further in each level of reality.

Hospital visits to Carol's mother

Level of Reality	Indicator	Question	What you are noticing
Fundamental	Meaning	What is important about this?	Carol and her mother know the church in general, and I in particular, support them, care for them.
Strategic	Direction	Where am I headed?	Congregants know I will support them in their times of need.

Everyday	Action	What needs to be done?	Continue to listen to Carol; she needs an outlet and even though I don't like being the target, I know she's just scared. Continue to set clear expectations with other parishioners of what they can expect from us.

As you look at *hospital visits with Carol's mother* now, what do you see that you didn't see before?

I was taking this so personally. I hadn't thought about how scared Carol must be.

What is the next step?

- Forgive myself for not thinking of Carol first.

- Continue to visit, be available for Carol—maybe ask her if it's OK to check in by phone while keeping my published visiting schedule.

- Going forward, think of the family, not just the person in the hospital.

Question #3: What Do I Need to Say Yes to? Say No To?

With so many competing calls for our time and attention, we may find ourselves operating on autopilot. When we're on autopilot, we abdicate control of our choices and allow ourselves to be buffeted by other forces, worrying about other people's demands and the pressures of *shoulds*.

As a result, we lose focus. We waste energy complaining, leaving us too spent to address the things we want or need to focus on. Our switch becomes permanently stuck in the On position.

To increase your ability to switch Off, establish clear boundaries between Off and On. Remember every action or reaction—even no action—is a choice. Every time we say *yes* to one thing, we say *no* to another. In the same way, if we say *no* to something, we say *yes* to something else. When we make conscious and intentional choices, we're better able to reclaim our sense of control.

Examples

Our whole world runs 24/7 now. I don't take vacation. I don't have downtime. I feel guilty when I do.

When this well-intentioned pastor says *no* to vacation and downtime, she says *yes* to feeling tired and overwhelmed. Perhaps this choice serves her and her congregation. Our guess is this devoted minister will not be able to sustain her current pace.

I don't know when to say no. The congregation has reasonable expectations. I don't want to say no because I love what I do.

35

Even when we love what we do, we must use our Off Switch on a regular basis. Without self-care, we are likely to face burnout and then cannot be of service to anyone. An extreme yet true example is a minister we know who loved his congregation and worked around the clock supporting his community. Unfortunately, he passed away suddenly at the age of forty-two from a massive heart attack. While his family and congregation took comfort in their belief that he had gone to meet his Maker, they also shared sadness for the loss of his potential impact, guidance, and love.

Like his colleague in the first example, when this person said *yes* to one more thing for the congregation—even though he liked it—he said *no* to something else. Perhaps he said no to being home with his family for dinner or going to the gym.

We don't know which decisions are "right" or "good." The merits of these decisions are relevant only to the individuals, their families, and their congregations. The important thing is making the choices rather than the choices making you. Because not making a decision is a decision to leave things just as they are.

The first step to regaining our sense of control is to become aware of the choices we're making, whether consciously or on autopilot. As you become more aware of the choices you are making and the circumstances you are tolerating, you may decide you need to make different choices. Maybe you can't change your circumstances, but by consciously and intentionally choosing the way you approach them, you reclaim control of your experience.

Tool #3: Your Boundary Analysis

Step 1: Jot down your first reaction to these questions.

What are you tolerating?

What are you saying yes to?

What are you saying no to?

Step 2:

What do you need to say yes to?

What do you need to say no to?

Step 3:

How will these commitments help you find your Off Switch and help you use it?

Figure 17 – Finding and Using Your Off Switch: Establishing Boundaries

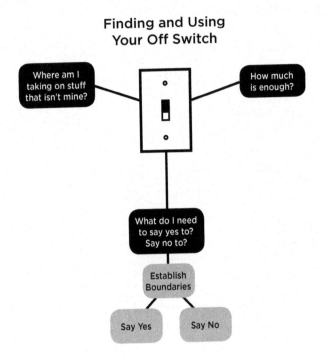

Finding and Using Your Off Switch

Case Vignette

Deborah is the rector at the local church. While Deborah has good relationships with almost everyone in the congregation, Stan poses a challenge. He loves to boast about how he never comes to services, which is bad enough, but even worse is his list of "helpful suggestions." Deborah is pretty good at finding important things to do in her office or in the sanctuary when Stan comes to pick his kids up from church. But Stan has a knack for grocery shopping at the same time she does. And he always seems to have his suggestion list appended to his grocery list. Deborah is tired of trying to dodge him; it takes a lot of energy and she feels like a fraud, since she is sure a "real" priest wouldn't do something so petty. She is tired of complaining about him, and she is sure her husband, spiritual director, and secretary are equally tired of her complaining.

Figure 18 – Deborah's Boundary Analysis

Step 1: Jot down your first reaction to these questions.

What are you tolerating?

- I am tolerating the uncertainty and annoyance of Stan.

What are you saying yes to?

- I am saying yes to allowing Stan to determine my mood/behavior.

What are you saying no to?

- I am saying no to taking control of the situation, even taking an active part in it.

Step 2:

What do you need to say yes to?

- I need to say yes to being active in setting limits with Stan, stating when I'm receptive to his suggestions or when it's not a good time.

- I need to say yes to really listening to Stan when it is a good time. While I don't like the way Stan delivers his message, I think he offers his suggestions with good intent.

What do you need to say no to?

- I need to say no to being passive.

Step 3:

How will these commitments help you find your Off Switch and help you use it?

- I will be able to use my Off Switch when I am out and about around town. I won't be worrying about whether or not I will run into Stan, experiencing that clenching feeling in my stomach or having to duck into the next aisle at the grocery story to avoid him. I will say yes to meeting with him in the office.

Are You Focusing on What You Can Control?

When we consider where we spend our energy, we're often shocked to see the things we cannot control get significantly more of our attention than the things we can. Where do you spend your time, attention, and energy?

Tool #4: Your Control Analysis

Draw two columns, and label one Can Control and the other Cannot Control. Complete the chart based on what you are facing right now. (Consider these two independent lists; you do not need to have corresponding entries in both columns. We put the columns next to each other so it's easy to work with them.)

Can Control:	Cannot Control:

> Which list gets more of your attention?
>
> Going forward, what will you do?

Figure 19 — Deborah's Control Analysis

Can Control:	Cannot Control:
• What I say to Stan	• What Stan will say to me
• My reaction to Stan	• When Stan will appear
• Really listening to Stan	• What people will think if they see me talking with Stan
• How I feel about my behavior toward Stan	
• Worrying about when Stan will appear	• How long Stan will talk

Which list gets more of your attention?

The Cannot Control list—especially what other people think.

Going forward, what will you do?

Notice when I worry about running into Stan. Remember to breathe and be present rather than worry about what might happen.

Your Personal Plan

In this book you have been introduced to four tools to help you find and use your Off Switch:

- Tool #1: Your Role Analysis
- Tool #2: Your Reality Check
- Tool #3: Your Boundary Analysis
- Tool #4: Your Control Analysis

On the following page, we introduce a fifth tool, Your Personal Action Plan, to help you turn what you have learned into real change. In Part III, you will find the tools grouped together for easy reference. Use them to help you identify the issues that keep you switched on and to create a customized plan to switch off.

Figure 20 – Finding and Using Your Off Switch: The Whole Model

Finding and Using Your Off Switch

- Where am I taking on stuff that isn't mine?
- How much is enough?
- Key Roles
- Levels of Reality
  - Outer
  - Inner
  - Ghost
  - Everyday
  - Strategic
  - Fundamental
- Role Challenges
  - Individual not the role
  - Poorly occupied
  - Outer role confusion
  - Innter role confusion
  - Role creep
  - Role changes
  - Role nausea
- What do I need to say yes to? Say no to?
- Action   Direction   Meaning
- Establish Boundaries
  - Say Yes
  - Say No

Tool #5: Your Personal Action Plan for Finding and Using Your Off Switch

What have you learned from your roles analysis, your reality check, establishing your boundaries, and your control analysis?

Building on what you learned, what are the top priorities requiring your attention to find and use your Off Switch?

Personal Action Plan

Specific Objective:

Action to Be Taken and Target Date:

SMART Goals

SMART goals are used often in corporate strategic planning, and they can be just as useful in personal strategic planning. Often people set vague goals and then wonder why they don't accomplish what they set out to do. The SMART formula helps us create precise goals, which most often become achieved goals.

SMART is an acronym:

S stands for specific. What precisely will you do?

M stands for measurable. How will you know when you've accomplished your objective?

A is for action-oriented. Is this something you can do?

R is for realistic. For example, eating an elephant for dinner is certainly action-oriented, but is it realistic?

T is for time-sensitive. When will you get this done? For some goals, your time line may be very short; others may take an extended period.

PART II

THE OFF-SWITCH RETREAT

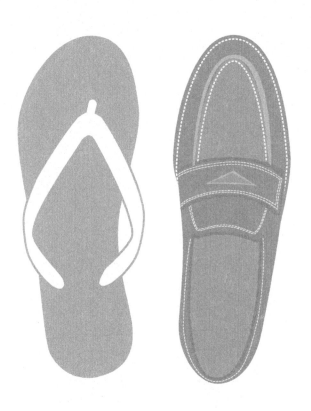

THE OFF-SWITCH RETREAT

This story illustrates how to use the Off Switch questions and exercises in this book. As with the vignettes in previous sections, the characters and examples in this story are drawn from themes from interviews with active congregational clergy. Some of them will be spot-on for your situation; some will not resonate personally. We urge you not to be distracted by the details but instead to use them as a model for finding your Off Switch in your own circumstances.

Howard groaned to himself.

A minister for twenty-eight years, Howard had come to this retreat eager to find support from clergy who were also in the last third of their careers. To learn from colleagues who'd been in the trenches and could speak from experience.

But the joke was on him, Howard thought. The one participant he really didn't want to be paired with was, naturally, his partner for the next two days.

Howard prided himself on being open-minded. After all, the 1960s were formative years for him. His older siblings were active in civil rights and war protests. Live and Let Live, quickly followed by I'm OK, You're OK, became mottos of the times.

But deep down, part of Howard was a holdover from a previous era. Although he hated to admit it even to himself, in his heart of hearts, Howard had strong opinions of the way clergy should behave. And much of what he thought clergy should not do was standing right in front of him: his partner for the next two days.

From his full height of six foot four, Howard stared down. They had nothing in common. His partner's hair looked as if she hadn't touched it since she got out of bed. Although she was wearing only one earring in each ear, he could see four vacant holes in her left ear. Her clothing, while modest, was... *bohemian* was the best description he could come up with. During introductions, he learned she'd been out of seminary for only three years. Howard believed young clergy have much to offer, but really, how could working with this young woman provide the shot in the arm he and his career needed?

Looking up at Howard, Kylie wondered the same thing. He seemed like a nice guy and all, but she'd come to this retreat to get away, to get a fresh perspective on the challenges she faced. Kylie worked with "a nice enough guy," and he was driving her crazy!

Kylie appreciated the challenges men like Howard faced. The world had changed since they were ordained. Their early role models had been men who inspired awe; they and their peers were men (and a few women) of authority. But now congregations, especially the young people every church and synagogue was trying to attract, wanted clergy who were approachable.[3]

---

3. We are grateful to Rabbi Michael Feshbach for the concept of awe, authority, and approachability.

Yeah, Kylie got their struggles, but "nice enough guys" like this were limiting what she could do and in turn, holding back the congregation.

Accepting that the fates had paired them up, each took a breath and tried to put his or her assumptions aside.

"Did you do the pre-work?" Kylie asked, not sure where else to start. Howard nodded, taking out the spiral notebook he'd bought for the retreat. "Me, too," she said, opening her iPad. She caught Howard trying to control his facial expression. They both smiled, acknowledging that their choice of writing material was only one of many differences between them.

They'd been asked to complete a worksheet before coming to the retreat. As the retreat leader, Eve, sent them off for their first pairs' discussion, she urged them to focus their conversation on what they learned from the exercises rather than walking through their answers to each question.

"Well, what did you learn?" Howard asked. While he still didn't know what Kylie could possibly teach him, he was eager to coach and help her.

Kylie scrunched up her face as she collected her thoughts. "I'm...not sure," she said slowly, gazing over Howard's shoulder as if she were trying to read the answer on the wall behind him. "When I came to the congregation, everyone told me how exciting it was for me to bring fresh ideas, new people—young people."

Howard raised an eyebrow at "everyone."

"Really. Everyone. It was almost freakish, as if they were all reading from the same script. But yes, everyone."

49

"I've only been doing this for twenty-nine years, but I find it hard to believe a congregation exists where everyone agrees on anything," Howard responded.

Kylie set her jaw and leveled a look at Howard.

"But I'll concede the point," he said quickly. "That's great. Everyone's on the same page."

"They say the same thing, but I don't think they mean it."

"Now that I believe," Howard said.

"But it's all so vague. Ed, my senior—he's . . ." Kylie hesitated. Howard reminded her so much of her boss she felt as if she were offending him. But when Howard didn't react, she continued. "Honestly, I think he feels threatened by me."

Now Howard winced. Imperceptibly, Kylie shrank back, concerned she'd offended him.

"Keep going," Howard encouraged.

She looked uncomfortable. "Even though I don't know him, I suspect I have a lot in common with Ed." Kylie's sheepish smile betrayed her. They both hesitated.

"Look," said Howard, "blunt and direct isn't really my style, but—"

"I love blunt and direct!" Kylie broke in.

"Yes, I figured that." He took a deep breath. "I'll admit working with you this weekend wasn't my first choice." She nodded knowingly. Howard continued, "I was hoping to be paired with someone like Ed." She blushed. "But we're here together, so let's just say what we need to."

Kylie picked up where she left off. "So the ultimate question of the homework was: where am I taking on stuff that isn't mine? As I look over my answers, I just don't know. I feel as if . . . maybe my outer and inner roles are in conflict." It was more of a question than a statement.

"I was hired to be an innovator," Kylie continued. "I think of it as an inner role. I mean, my outer role is to teach, preach, visit, you know. But every time I try something new, I'm told it's too risky, 'too much too fast.'

"Ed wants me to submit my sermons to him a few days before I preach. I'm fine with that: he's a gifted preacher, and I'm glad to learn from him. But he doesn't teach! He'll say, 'This isn't the time for X' or 'I don't think the congregation will respond well to Y.' When I ask him how to say things differently or what topics or timing he thinks are appropriate, he doesn't answer. He'll hem and haw or say, 'We'll talk about it later.' But we don't. I used to ask to make appointments for feedback and suggestions, but I stopped because I was so frustrated."

Howard looked thoughtful. He loved coaching young clergy on their sermons. Maybe he and Ed weren't so alike.

"So what are you taking on that's not yours?" he asked, turning her back to the original question.

She paused to consider it, relieved to have the beginnings of a rant stopped. After a few minutes, she said, "I'm stuck."

"Maybe that's it!" Howard said, somewhat surprised at himself. Kylie brightened, not sure what he meant but eager for a fresh insight. "Maybe you are taking on 'being stuck.' I may not know you very well at this point, but you don't strike me as a person who would sign on to fill the role of 'stuck.'"

Kylie turned the idea over in her mind. "Maybe.... I need to digest that one. What about you? Where are you taking on stuff that isn't yours?"

"I struggled with this too. As I looked at my duties, they seemed like all the things a person in my position is supposed to do: teach, preach, visit the sick, weddings."

"The usual," they said in unison.

"It was the questions about role nausea and ghosts that stopped me in my tracks. I mean"—he looked around to make sure no one else could hear what he was about to say—"I love what I do," he said with a look that didn't match his words. "But I'm so sick of being the only person who can make a decision."

Figure 21 – Howard's Role Analysis

Role Identification
List all of your outer roles. • Teacher • CEO/Decision-maker • Mentor
List all of your inner roles • Leader • Sympathetic ear/shoulder to cry on.
What ghosts are affecting your role/congregation? Dr. Miller, who led my grandparents' congregation Brother Mike, my sister's best friend from college, who led protests on every subject imaginable but always turned the other cheek
Where have you become too closely identified with a role? Decision maker. Everyone seems afraid to do anything or make a decision without me.
Poorly Occupied Roles Truster. I trust my congregants and staff, but they don't really trust themselves—or maybe they don't trust me. So I get dragged into meetings and conversations I don't need to be in.

Role Confusion

I didn't think I was confused, but now that I think about it, maybe I'm confused about what my role is if I let others start making more decisions and do the things that have been part of my responsibility. All of this is making me question what the role of senior pastor should be! I don't know the first thing about business, but people see me as the CEO! I think volunteers (and to some extent, staff) are confused about where they get to make decisions and where I need to make them.

Role Changes

The role of "visionary" needs to emerge. No one is thinking about the congregation for the long term. Will we grow? If so, how? If not, what will happen? I like this kind of visioning, but I'll be gone in a few years.

Role Nausea

I'm sick of the business end. I wish I had time to study new texts or old texts in a new way, or work with a new group of congregants—maybe those in hospice.

Where are you taking on stuff that isn't yours due to role challenges?

The longer I'm the only one making decisions, the harder it will be for the congregants to feel it's *their* congregation, and in turn, the harder it will be for a new pastor to fit in.

Figure 22 – Kylie's Role Analysis

Role Identification
List all of your outer roles. • Young people outreach • Teacher • Sermon-giver • Social action coordinator
List all of your inner roles • Student • Innovator
What ghosts are affecting your role/congregation? "This is the way we've always done it."
Where have you become too closely identified with a role? Young person
Poorly Occupied Roles Mentor
Role Confusion I don't know what role Ed wants to play. He did everything before I came into this newly created position. He said he wanted help, but he doesn't seem to want to let anything go.
Role Changes I've become the "complainer." That needs to change.

> ### Role Nausea
>
> I'm sick of coming up with ideas that constantly get shot down.
>
> *Where are you taking on stuff that isn't yours due to role challenges?*
>
> I feel as if I'm not doing my job due to role confusion. I don't know what my job is supposed to be! I hate to think my frustration is negatively affecting anyone else's experience at church. But maybe I've been too absorbed in my own "complainer" role to notice my impact on others.

* * *

Eve, the retreat leader, called them back. As they took their chairs in the group circle, Eve wrote three words on the whiteboard.

Figure 23 – The 3 Rs of the Off Switch

> *Relax*
>
> *Reflect*
>
> *Refresh*

"Well, how are we doing on our three Rs?" she asked. The hint of a smile on her face blossomed into a full grin as the participants rolled their eyes and some even groaned.

"I'm more tense than before we started," said Charles, a priest from a large church in a large city.

His discussion partner, Walter, a minister from a small town, nodded. "I feel the same way. Our roles have some similar qualities, but our frustrations are completely different. But as you called us back, we both said, 'Great—now we have a better idea of why we're frustrated, which seems to have simply upped our frustration level!'"

The entire group chuckled.

"Terrific." Eve's smile somehow grew even larger. "That's just where I expected you to be at this point.

"We're going to switch gears a little now. As we discussed at the beginning, the purpose of this retreat is to help you reflect on your circumstances, using some new tools. Throughout this retreat we'll be looking at three broad questions.

1. Where am I taking on stuff that isn't mine?
2. How much is enough?
3. What do I need to say yes to? And its cousin, what do I need to say no to?

"So far, we've gotten a good start on number one. What is different for you now that you've had time to delve into this question both in your pre-work and in your pairs?"

Alan, probably the most seasoned member of the group, raised his hand. "These exercises confirmed what I already suspected. I'm very clear on my role. I've been doing it for thirty years. I think I've finally figured it out," he said with a half-smirk, half-grin. "The problem is our young staff. Two years out of seminary and they think they know everything and are entitled to do everything. It took me years to earn those honors, to learn to anticipate the needs of the congregation, to hone my skills. Who do these young people think they are?"

Howard tried to stifle a laugh and keep his expression neutral as he imagined his childhood pastor, Dr. Miller, sitting in

Alan's chair. As Kylie all but jumped out of her chair to take on Alan, a small hand signal from Eve put her back in her seat. Eve turned to Alan.

"Thanks, Alan." Kylie seethed as Eve continued, "That can't be easy for you." Alan nodded. "What did you discover about Question 1? Where are you taking on stuff that isn't yours?"

"I don't think I am," he said respectfully and emphatically. "I just wish these young people would remember their position is 'assistant' for a reason and do their jobs."

Kylie looked at Eve expectantly, waiting for her to read Alan the riot act. Instead, Eve simply said, "That's great."

Howard glanced at Kylie as she deflated. Eve looked at the rest of the group. "The invitation is to keep your mind open. At the end of our time together, some of you will find yourselves exactly where you are right now. Some of you will find new answers, or at least new possibilities, as we continue to explore.

"And you, sir," she said to Alan, "have brought us to exactly where we need to be. We are going to break for the day. It's an opportunity for you to continue to relax, reflect, and refresh independently. Use your Off Switch in whatever way works for you. The weather is expected to be lovely this evening if you prefer the outdoors."

Eve began passing out papers, saying, "Sometime between now and when we reconvene in the morning, you have some homework to complete. When you get back with your partner you will be using your responses to the question, 'How much is enough?'"

* * *

As she entered the room the next morning, Eve heard a participant lament, "This is a tough question."

"You mean the last one wasn't?" cracked Adam, one of two rabbis in the group.

As the chuckles subsided, Eve said, "Good morning, everyone. 'How much is enough?' can be a tough question. We're bombarded by messages of 'more, more, more.' 'Whatever you do, it's not enough.' 'You're not enough.'

"The question presumes there's an easy answer: X is enough. But really, is there such a thing as enough sick visits, counseling conversations, or whatever? Defining enough based on the measurable to-dos of everyday reality causes most of us to hesitate using our Off Switch.

"So this next section tweaks the question. We use **the three levels of reality** to answer the question 'How do I make peace with feeling that whatever I do isn't enough?' We reflect on our values or passion at the fundamental level, and on our vision, hopes, and fears at the strategic level to inform our choices in everyday reality.

"Given limited time—even 24/7 is limited—and an unlimited list of things to do, we have to make choices. With so many masters to serve, it's complicated! So we have another tool for pulling apart some of the competing demands.

"The three levels of reality serve several purposes. First, we need all three levels.

"Too much everyday reality—too much focus on doing, doing, doing—and people burn out. Too much strategic or fundamental and nothing gets done. In the best of times, the meaning or purpose of the fundamental level infuses our vision and elevates the doing in everyday reality.

"The very best leaders, teachers, and preachers navigate all three levels seamlessly, and we need to help other people do the same: connect the dots among why, what, and how.

"Second, this framework also reminds us each person has a preferred level of reality. No one is best or 'right.' But knowing someone's preferred level and meeting them on that level, rather than on our own, leads to better connection and communication.

"Your homework from last night was designed to help you address the frustrations that surfaced in the roles exercises. The goal is not to fix a problem, but to look for new ways to approach it. Or perhaps"—Eve looked at Alan—"new ways of having old conversations."

With that, she sent them back into their pairs armed with their responses from their homework.

Figure 24 — Howard's Reality Check

List the many parts of your outer and inner roles where it seems as if, no matter what you do, it's not enough.

1. Decision maker. No matter how many times I encourage people to go with their own decisions, they keep coming back to me.
2. Visiting with members and visitors before and after services.
3. Reviewing church finances, insurance needs, and other business matters (why don't they teach this in seminary?)
4. Preparing for adult education—sure I can wing it, but it doesn't feel right

Pick one to explore further in each level of reality.

Rethinking the decision-making process in our church.

Level of Reality	Indicator	Question	What you are noticing
Fundamental	Meaning	What's important about this?	Several things. First, selfishly, I think I'm a bottle-neck, and that makes me feel guilty. Second, it's making others dependent on me, which limits the congregation's po-tential to try new things and grow.
Strategic	Direction	Where am I headed?	I want more time for activities that have more mean-ing for me person-ally. If I step out of the role of decision maker on certain issues, our lay leaders will have a chance to test their ideas. And I'll have more energy for the decisions that really need my attention.

Everyday	Volume	What needs to be done?	A review of what decisions need to be made and assign various people to be in charge.

As you look at _decision-making_ now, what do you see that you didn't see before?

If something is going to change, I need to initiate the change.

What is the next step?

- I will sit down with a pad and paper and make a list of the decisions I need to be involved in and the ones I can delegate.

- Based on my list I will start to educate my staff and volunteers to reset expectations for decision-making.

Figure 25 – Kylie's Reality Check

List the many parts of your outer and inner roles where it seems as if, no matter what you do, it's not enough.

1. Change agent. I come up with ideas until I'm blue in the face, and I try to "sell" them in different ways, but nothing works.
2. Junior pastor. Ed won't let me forget the "junior" part. I don't get a chance to try on the "pastor" part.

Pick one to explore further in each level of reality.

Change agent

Level of Reality	Indicator	Question	What you are noticing
Fundamental	Meaning	What's important about this?	The existence of the congregation. Ed and some of the longtime members are so committed to doing things the way they've always done them, they're missing how the needs of the community have changed.
Strategic	Direction	Where am I headed?	If the congregation doesn't make some changes, I'm afraid it will continue to decline and may die over the next twenty to twenty-five years.

Everyday	Volume	What needs to be done?	So much! I think the first thing I should do is have conversations with Ed and the congregation leaders about my long-term concerns.

As you look at _being a change agent_ now, what do you see that you didn't see before?

Before I did this exercise, I was seeing this only as an issue of my career development. I realize now this is much bigger than that. I need to sit and really think about the role I am in. Maybe the change-agent role should be assigned to someone more senior. Maybe a longtime lay leader?

What is the next step?

- Sit down and think about my inner and outer roles as they exist today.

- Identify what I think needs to evolve.

- Schedule a meeting with Ed to discuss.

"As you look at your responses, what occurs to you?" Eve had suggested they start with this question, so Howard did, although he found it awkward and a bit forced. "It occurs to me we were both caught up in ourselves," he said, smiling.

Kylie agreed. "I love the church, our congregation, and the denomination. I want other people to love them, too. And I want these institutions to be here in five, ten, a hundred years.

That's why we need to make changes—because what worked beautifully in the past isn't working now.

"Plus this is a new role. I mean, I knew that going in, but I thought I could make it work, that it would be easy. I...we may be able to make it work, but maybe not so easily. It sounds naïve but I hadn't thought it through, that people would have different expectations."

Kylie looked thoughtful. "I had all of these ideas in my head, but I could see only the roadblocks. Now, looking at them in black and white, I know exactly what to do in"—she glanced at her notes—"everyday reality."

"Now I guess it's my turn," he said. "I don't know, our church runs pretty well. I have nothing to complain about."

Kylie waited expectantly, since clearly he was complaining.

"I sometimes feel too relaxed. I don't plan to retire for another eight to ten years, but the thought of the same old, same old for the next ten years is depleting, not refreshing."

Howard continued, "Our congregation is also caught up in 'This is how we've always done it.' I hadn't realized it but I created it!" A guilty look flashed across his face. "I like being in charge. I confess, I like being the guy people turn to. And if I'm really honest, I admit I haven't wanted to let go of some of my responsibilities because people might forget me or think I'm irrelevant if I don't have at least one finger in everything. But it's draining me. And it's also exhausting the congregation."

Eve dropped in at that moment. "That's why the three levels are so important," she emphasized. "A vision infused with your values is a compelling vision."

Howard looked around the room. As he turned back to Kylie, he looked excited but afraid to get his hopes up. "I'd trade places with Esther, the hospice chaplain," he said, pointing to another member of the class. "I've visited congregants in hospice, but really putting time and attention there—that seems meaningful.…" His voice trailed off as he got a faraway look in his eyes.

"Maybe I'd take a little bit from a couple of people," he said, bringing himself back. He looked at two participants across the room. "Carol and Jonah talked about their study group. I'd love to participate in a study group on some of the texts I haven't read in a while." He leveled his gaze at Kylie. "I'd like to mentor or coach someone like you. Or maybe a young rabbi or an imam. I bet they could teach me a thing or two."

Glancing at her notes, Kylie asked, "What needs to happen?"

A hint of a grin played at the corners of Howard's mouth as he thought about the question. "I need to decide what things I need to be involved in and select a few lay leaders to handle the areas I can and want to delegate. My fear of being irrelevant—it's real, it's there, but honestly, the chances are practically zero. The congregation would love to have me take on some of these things, especially if it will keep me from leaving, or worse, staying and being cranky."

He thought some more. "I just didn't know I wanted these things until we had this conversation."

"How do you feel now?" asked Eve as she walked by.

"Refreshed."

Kylie and Howard decided to sit outside for their last round of exercises. They agreed to take a fifteen-minute walk around the grounds before getting to work.

Eve had introduced the concept of yes/no. "Whenever we say yes to something, by definition, we're saying no to something else," she'd said. It made perfect sense, but Howard had never thought about it quite that way before.

They'd tried working through the exercises in different ways: talking first, one taking notes as the other spoke. They'd decided to jot their own notes before talking this time.

"So? Whatcha got?" Kylie asked.

Howard handed her his paper as she gave him her iPad.

Figure 26 – Howard's Boundary Analysis

Step 1:

Jot down your first reaction to these questions.

What are you tolerating?

- I'm tolerating unsatisfying parts of my role expanding to fill the time, crowding out room for parts that excite me.

What are you saying yes to?

- I am saying yes to the idea that I need to keep doing things exactly as I've been doing them for the last thirty years. My assumption is that what's worked in the past will continue to work in the future.

What are you saying no to?

- I'm saying no to change.

Step 2:

What do you need to say yes to?

- I need to say yes to expanding my idea of what I "should" do and what I have time for. I need to say yes to the idea that the congregation and I are both in different places from when I arrived thirty years ago. And therefore we need something different.

What do you need to say no to?

- I need to say no to worrying that other people might get upset. Maybe they will, but I can deal with it. But they probably won't.

Step 3:

How will these commitments help you find your Off Switch and help you use it?

- A few years ago, I would have had a different answer to this question. I think I'm learning that an Off Switch for me, at this point in my career, isn't about doing less—it isn't about time. It's about finding activities that have more meaning.

Figure 27 – Kylie's Boundary Analysis

Step 1:

Jot down your first reaction to these questions.

What are you tolerating?

- I'm tolerating being frustrated every day. I now I realize I've allowed frustration to turn into martyrdom.

What are you saying yes to?

- I am shocked, but I realize I have been saying yes to the inner role of "stuck."
- I'm saying yes to my being right all the time.

What are you saying no to?

- I'm saying no to learning something useful from my current position and my relationship with Ed.

Step 2:

What do you need to say yes to?

- I need to say yes to the possibility that I can learn something from my frustration.

What do you need to say no to?

- I need to say no to complaining, even when the complaining is only in my head.

Step 3:

How will these commitments help you find your Off Switch and help you use it?

- I never realized how exhausting being "right" is. I also now see I've marginalized some of my top values, like respect. I don't respect Ed, but I hadn't thought about it in terms of being out of alignment with my values.

Howard said, "I hadn't realized how much of my day has been filled with things I've been doing because I always did them that way. I need to say yes to really looking at all the day-to-day tasks I do and see if I'm still the right person to do them. There are some tasks that probably don't need to be done at all, but I do them religiously!" They both smiled. "If I dumped them, I'd have a lot more energy for the studying, mentoring, and hospice work we talked about earlier."

As Howard started to say something else, Kylie cut him off. "I know—you're going to tell me I need to use an Off Switch even though I'm young. But I practice yoga, I do a lot of things to refresh."

"When we first met, I probably would have told you that," Howard said. "But I've learned a lot about both of us in the short time we've been working together. We both like to ask questions and let others come up with their own answers, rather than telling others what we think. But I will tell you about my own experience...which you, of course, can choose to ignore.

"When I was a new minister I never thought about an Off Switch. I'm not sure I seriously thought about it for much of my career. About ten years ago, I noticed my energy level changing and I began to wish I could turn off, but that's when cell phones and e-mail became mainstream, and I got tired of being expected to be available all the time.

"Rather than fighting the idea of an Off Switch, embrace that you're already using it. Yoga is a form of an Off Switch: it's relaxing, reflecting, and refreshing all at once! And as your career evolves, you might need something else. Just don't forget to have some kind of Off Switch practice. If you don't make time for it, no one will make it for you."

Figure 28 – Howard's Control Analysis

Howard's Control Analysis	
Can Control:	*Cannot Control:*
• What I say yes to • What I say no to • How I respond to other people's reactions	• Other people's reactions • If I push others to make decisions, will they step up?
Which list gets more of your attention?	
Cannot control list.	
Going forward, what will you do?	
Remember I CAN control what I say yes/no to, and focus on those questions.	

Figure 29 – Kylie's Control Analysis

Kylie's Control Analysis	
Can Control:	*Cannot Control:*
• What I do • My attitude • What inner roles I choose	• What Ed does • How others feel about Ed or me

Which list gets more of your attention?
Cannot control list.
Going forward, what will you do?
Choose a new inner role which will bring me a new attitude. Not sure what yet...

"I'm pretty sure I could deal with those pressures," Kylie said, "but I just don't see how I can make things work with Ed. He's an energy vampire."

She looked up from her notes with tears of frustration. "I have tried everything. I've talked to my friends, my family, my teachers. I've tried all of their suggestions to forge a better relationship with Ed, but nothing has worked. I'm sick of complaining about it, and I'm sure others are, too. And I don't want to quit this position, but I don't know what else to do."

"Maybe a fresh set of ears can give you a different perspective. Give me an example of what you've said to Ed," Howard suggested.

Kylie took a deep breath, trying not to take out her frustrations on Howard. She knew he was trying to help.

"Sermons. That was my favorite class in seminary. When Ed was on vacation last summer, I gave two sermons. The congregation loved one, and the other, not so much." She smiled with chagrin. "But it was so interesting to hear what resonated, what didn't. As much as I loved preaching, I loved the feedback even more. Several members, especially some of the longtime members, said they hoped to hear me preach more.

"When Ed came back, I said something to him, but he blew it off."

Howard remarked, "You said 'something.' Tell me specifically what you said."

"I don't remember exactly. It was a year ago, but I think I said, 'I loved preaching. It opened a whole new conversation between me and many of the members.' And he said, 'That's nice,' and that was the end of it."

Howard's face lit up. "It just occurred to me why some of my conversations end up in mess too. You made a statement, 'I loved preaching,' but you didn't ask to give the sermon more often. You didn't make a request. Now you are mad because Ed responded to what you did say. He can't anticipate what you didn't say."

Kylie glared at him with the look he usually received only from his sixteen-year-old daughter.

"Look, it would have been great if Ed had gone a step further," Howard admitted. "In a perfect world, perhaps he would be more active about finding opportunities for you. But in fairness, he can't read your mind, and he's got a lot on his plate."

Kylie nodded, digesting his words, if not fully accepting them. Howard continued, "Since Ed's not here, I'm not going to weigh in on what his responsibility is, but you haven't done everything yet to improve your relationship. You've hinted, but you haven't come out and asked for what you want. Calmly figure out what you want and clearly ask for it. If he says no or ignores your request, then you can be mad and self-righteous."

Howard pointed to the last set of exercises.

Figure 30 — Howard's Action Plan for Finding and Using His Off Switch

What have you learned from your role analysis, your reality check, establishing your boundaries, and your control analysis?

I've learned that I'm the one who has placed the limits on myself. A lot of the issues I complain about are within my control to change, by either adjusting what I do or how I approach what I do. Many of the tasks of my outer roles can be delegated. Some will feel very different as I shift from seeing them as everyday-reality drudgery to fundamental-based service. And others probably won't bother me as they take up a smaller percentage of my time, when I add newer, more meaningful tasks to my schedule.

Building on what you learned, what are the top priorities requiring your attention to find and use your Off Switch?

- More reflecting at the fundamental level, really connecting what motivates me with what I do every day.

- Taking responsibility for what I say yes to and what I say no to. I didn't realize how passive I've been about this.

Personal Action Plan

Specific Objective:
More meaning

Action to Be Taken and Target Date:

- Call congregation member who's a social worker and ask what facilities could use additional pastoral counseling (May 1)

- Set up monthly counseling appointments (May 31)

- Write down what I want from a study partnership: what I hope to learn, how I'd like to set it up, and what I'll commit to (May 15)

- Identify three to five people I think would be good study partners (May 20)

- Contact them, set up first session (June 30)

Figure 31 — Kylie's Action Plan for Finding and Using Her Off Switch

What have you learned from your role analysis, your reality check, establishing your boundaries, and your control analysis?

I have learned that some of my frustrations may not be personal, as I have been feeling. I am starting to see a variety of forces are at play, and they may or may not have anything to do with me. Specifically, roles (Ed was both the pastor and his own assistant before I was hired) and levels of reality—Ed and I operate on different levels.

Building on what you learned, what are the top priorities requiring your attention to find and use your Off Switch?

• My top priority is revisiting what's in my control (asking to preach more versus saying I enjoyed it) and what isn't (Ed might say no) and making sure I am doing what is within my control.

• My second priority is looking at my career from the fundamental and strategic levels of reality, then creating a plan in everyday reality. I've been trying to move the chess pieces without really knowing my game plan.

Personal Action Plan

Specific objective:
Regain control

Action to Be Taken and Target Date:

• Complete control analysis for what I want from Ed (May 1)

• Make specific requests of Ed (May 10)

• Create new SMART goals based on his answers (May 31)

• Develop a career vision: make appointment with seminary counselor (May 15)

As they came back to the group for the final time, Howard winked at Kylie and they shared a knowing glance. They both thought back to how disappointed they were initially with the pairings at the opening of the retreat. They were both comforted by the gift of supporting each other.

"You two look like a pair of cats who swallowed a nest of canaries," Adam remarked as Eve opened the debriefing session.

"Do we?" Howard looked simultaneously proud and surprised. "I think we both came into this retreat feeling pretty stuck." Kylie nodded. "And now I think it's safe to say we both feel unstuck. We know exactly what we're going to do when we get home."

"Although I think you have more confidence your action plan will work," said Kylie. "I know what I'm going to do, but I have no idea how it will turn out. My senior pastor may say no to everything, and then I don't know what I'll do."

"You can call me, and we'll start over," Howard whispered as Eve stood to address the group.

"How about the rest of you? Do you all have a clear action plan?" she asked.

"No!" cried Paula, a minister. "I'm still stuck. When I get back tomorrow, I have two funerals during the day and a wedding in the evening. I'm not taking on someone else's stuff—there isn't anyone else to do it! And I'd like to give the student pastor more time, but as I look out over the next month, all my hours are spoken for," she said, shaking her head and looking at her calendar. "Good thing my kids are grown. I don't know how y'all are supposed to do it," she said, looking at the young mothers in the group. "Y'all, too!" she added, waving at the young fathers.

"It would be nice if everyone had a breakthrough at these retreats, but sometimes that's not the case. What is different for you, Paula, since the retreat began?" Eve asked.

Paula thoughtfully looked over her notes from the exercises. "One thing that's different... I hadn't thought about how when I say yes to something, I automatically say no to something else and vice versa. I always thought I couldn't say no—it never occurred to me I was already doing it. I need to process that."

"Great! Now what is one action step you can take from this new thinking?" Eve prodded.

"I can... hmmm." Paula looked around the circle of colleagues somewhat sheepishly. "This probably sounds teeny-tiny to all of you, but it feels giant to me." She took in a deep breath. "Before I say yes to something, which I know I will, I will consider saying no." She exhaled forcefully.

"That's perfect, Paula," Eve said.

"One tiny step for mankind, one giant leap for Paula!" Adam, the rabbi who'd been partnered with Paula, congratulated her with one of his customary one-liners.

"Before you leave today, I'd like you both to make sure Paula's action plan includes a SMART goal on this commitment, along with follow-up between the two of you, OK?" said Eve.

"Roger," Adam responded. Paula nodded.

"And while the spotlight is on you, Adam, what's one highlight from your action plan?"

"We have to make some changes in my congregation's office, and I'm afraid the staff is going to have a hard time adjusting.

Until today I felt I had to figure out how to make work easier for them. Thinking about it kept me awake at night. All the staff personalities are all so different. What would work for one might upset another.

"I realize now that I've been tolerating an inefficient staff structure because it's easier than dealing with the potential conflict. I've been tolerating inefficiency because I'm afraid others will see I don't really know how to manage staff. I need to say yes to heartfelt, direct conversations with the staff, even if it means someone might get upset. I need to say no to thinking my answers are better than anyone else's." He looked sheepish. "That was hard to say. But I need to say no to having answers and say yes to asking and really listening."

"Alan, what about you?"

"Well, I said I was clear on my role, and I am clear on my outer role. For years, I did everything, I was chief cook and bottle-washer. Now that we have younger pastors coming in, I realize we haven't done a good job of defining their roles. I know what I think their outer roles are, but we've been fuzzy about defining it.

"I also realize that as my outer role has changed and new people have joined the staff, by definition my inner role has changed. I hadn't thought about that before. Even when I was fussin' right after we talked about roles—I guess this is how it all works together. I needed the three levels of reality to help me see my inner role has changed. I was so focused on everyday reality, I didn't understand inner roles. Now I see I have a whole congregation of inner roles in developing these people. No one developed me—it was sink or swim! Maybe I resented that.

But I need to say no to grumbling about whatever happened in the past. I need to say yes to how my role is changing.

"My action items are all around that," continued Alan. "I have a schedule for formalizing, at least informally, the role descriptions for our staff. I'm going to put my ideas down on paper, and then we'll talk about them as a group. Then I'll decide how it's all going to work," he concluded with a self-satisfied grin.

Walter, the minister, raised his hand. "I mentioned a lot of my challenges were about roles. After three years, I'm still relatively new in my church. The pastor emeritus served the congregation for forty years, and there's still some question about whether he's MWR—ministering while retired. I feel for him. He had the outer and inner role of leader for four decades. Now I have the outer role, and I'm working on earning the inner role and…it's not clear what the pastor emeritus role is. Deep down I think I've always known I've needed to initiate a series of conversations—with the pastoral council, with the congregation, with the emeritus pastor—about his role. I don't want to kick him to the curb, but his actions are diminishing my influence and leadership with the congregation.

"My action plan has several steps: making lists of who needs to talk to whom, clarifying what I want, drafting some conversation templates, and a bunch of other things. Alan said he'd be my accountability partner as I go through it."

"Walter, preparing for a retirement impacts the minister and the congregation. In fact, it's a whole different workshop." Eve turned to the others in the group to get some more responses to the retreat. Some had clear plans, some still needed to digest their new perspectives before making commitments.

All agreed to be in touch with their retreat partners to monitor their progress for the next six months.

"So you now know about the Off Switch. You have new tools for identifying the issues that keep you up, examining them in a fresh light, and giving yourself permission to address them in a way that will allow you to let go. As you turn off the lights at home, at your office, may you remember your own personal Off Switch. May you always remember you have the tools to relax, reflect, and refresh. May you give yourself the space to use them.

"Go in peace," Eve concluded.

PART III

YOUR PERSONAL ACTION PLAN

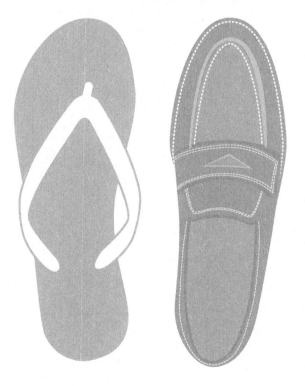

YOUR PERSONAL ACTION PLAN

I n Part I we introduced the model and the tools to find and use your Off Switch.

In Part II the retreat participants showed you how to use each tool to create Personal Action Plans.

Now it's your turn!

Grab a blank sheet of paper (or open a new digital document) and create your Personal Action Plan to switch off in three easy steps.

Step 1

What have you learned from your role analysis, your reality check, establishing your boundaries and your control analysis? Blank templates for each of these tools are on the following pages.

Step 2

Building on what you learned, what are the top priorities requiring your attention to find and use your Off Switch?

Step 3

List your specific objectives with the supporting action(s) and target date(s) to complete.

Congratulations! You are on your way to finding and using your Off Switch.

The Off-Switch Model

Finding and Using
Your Off Switch

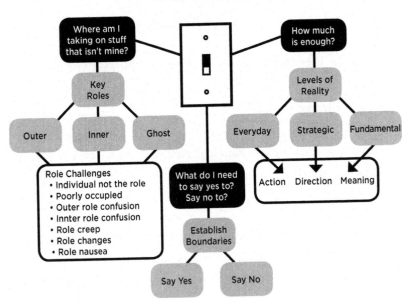

Tool #1: Your Role Analysis

Role Identification
List all of your outer roles.
List all of your inner roles.
What ghosts are affecting your role/congregation?
Where have you become too closely identified with a role?
Poorly Occupied Roles
Role Confusion
Role Changes
Role Nausea
Where are you taking on stuff that isn't yours due to role challenges?

Tool #2: Your Reality Check

List the many parts of your outer and inner roles where it seems as if, no matter what you do, it's not enough.

Pick one to explore further.

Issue:

Level of Reality	Indicator	Question	What you are noticing

As you look at the issue now, what do you see that you didn't see before?

What is the next step?

Tool #3: Your Boundary Analysis

Step 1: Jot down your first reaction to these questions.

What are you tolerating?

What are you saying yes to?

What are you saying no to?

Step 2:

What do you need to say yes to?

What do you need to say no to?

Step 3:

How will these commitments help you find your Off Switch and help you use it?

Tool #4: Your Control Analysis

Can Control:	Cannot Control:

Which list gets more of your attention?

Going forward, what will you do?

Tool #5: Your Personal Action Plan

What have you learned from your roles analysis, your reality check, establishing your boundaries, and your control analysis?
Building on what you learned, what are the top priorities requiring your attention to find and use your Off Switch?
Personal Action Plan
Specific Objective:
Action to Be Taken and Target Date:

CONCLUSION

Without the time to switch off on occasion, the most dedicated suffer from stress and even physical illness. If you are always On for others, the effects can seep into your relationships with family and friends, potentially leading to burn-out during your time with them.

In the book of Exodus we read, "Moses' father-in-law said to him, 'What you are doing isn't good. You will end up totally wearing yourself out, both you and these people who are with you. The work is too difficult for you. You can't do it alone'" (Exod 18:17-18). A few verses later we read,

> But you should also look among all the people for capable persons who respect God. They should be trustworthy and not corrupt.... They will share your load. If you do this and God directs you, then you will be able to endure. And all these people will be able to go back to their homes much happier. (Exod 18:21-23)

We believe this means Moses needed an Off Switch and, thanks to his father-in-law's coaching, he used it. We want the same for you. May you make sacred space in your holy work for reflecting, relaxing, and refreshing.

ACKNOWLEDGMENTS

Thank you to everyone who supported us in the process of bringing this book to fruition.

- Thank you to the clergy we interviewed for being so forthcoming, and to the people who introduced us to people we didn't know so we could broaden our insights.

- Thank you to the people who provided feedback on the drafts. You'll probably notice many of your ideas in these pages!

- Thank you to our new friends at Abingdon Press for your faith in this material and your immense help.

- Thank you to our friends and family who have been, and continue to be, our biggest cheerleaders.

; obtained

)03B/3/P